GEOGRAPHICS

VOLCANOES

Izzi Howell

W
FRANKLIN WATTS
LONDON·SYDNEY

Franklin Watts

First published in Great Britain in 2018 by The Watts Publishing Group

Copyright © The Watts Publishing Group 2018

Produced for Franklin Watts by
White-Thomson Publishing Ltd
www.wtpub.co.uk
01273 479982

Series Editor: Izzi Howell
Series Designer: Rocket Design (East Anglia) Ltd

Getty: ShaunWilkinson 7b, Stocktrek 8b, InterNetwork Media 9t, cgambaccini 10t, SalvagorGali 11, TatianaMironenko 12b, edella 13, jack0m 14t, blueringmedia 21t; NASA: Earth Sciences and Image Analysis, NASA-Johnson Space Center 21b, William L. Stefanov, NASA-JSC 29b; NOAA: Okeanos Explorer Program, Galapagos Rift Expedition 2011 14b, PMEL EOI Program 15b; Shutterstock: TyBy cover and title page, Jakinnboaz 6, Designua 7t, 18, 19t, 22, Kuryanovich Tatsiana 9b, etvulc 10c, Robert Crow 10b, Axel Wolf 12t, mapichai 15t, Lorelyn Medina 19c, Delpixel 19b, Mayboroda 20t, Hit1912 20b, Sentavio 23t, J. Helgason 23b, Natali Snailcat 24t, Rainer Lesniewski 25l, Byelikova Oksana 25r, saiko3p 26, Maridav 27t, Alejo Miranda 27b, Chattapat 28, VDOVINA ELENA 29t; Techtype: 4–5, 9c, 16–17.

All design elements from Shutterstock.

ISBN 978 1 4451 5559 3

Printed in China

Franklin Watts
An imprint of
Hachette Children's Group
Part of The Watts Publishing Group
Carmelite House
50 Victoria Embankment
London EC4Y 0DZ

An Hachette UK Company
www.hachette.co.uk
www.franklinwatts.co.uk

Contents

What are Volcanoes?

Volcanoes are holes in the Earth's surface where hot magma and gas from deep underground are released. Over time, volcanoes grow into tall mountains made from hardened lava and ash.

There are currently around 1,900 active volcanoes on Earth!

Mount St Helens
(page 9)

 Mount Fuji
(page 20)

 Mauna Loa
(page 21)

Mount Pinatubo
(page 8)

 Krakatoa
(page 24)

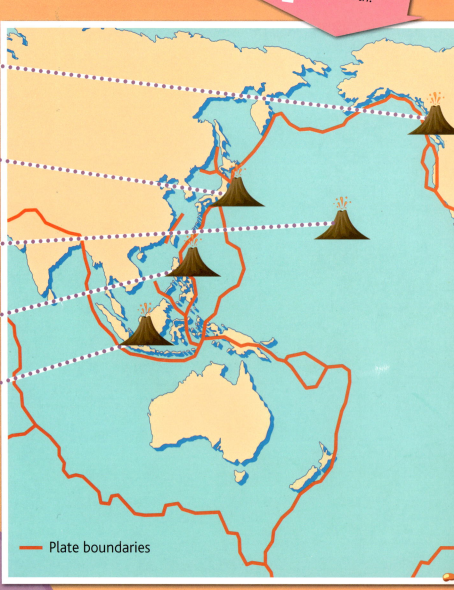

— Plate boundaries

Location

Volcanoes are often found along the boundaries of tectonic plates, where sections of the Earth's crust (outer layer) meet. Some volcanoes form at hotspots – places where magma inside the Earth is particularly hot. There are volcanoes on every continent on Earth.

Eruption

Active volcanoes sometimes erupt (see pages 10–11). Lava flows down the sides of the volcano. Gas and ash are released into the air. When the lava hardens, it forms rock.

Active, dormant, extinct

Active volcanoes still erupt frequently or are expected to erupt soon. Dormant volcanoes are unlikely to erupt again. Extinct volcanoes will never erupt again. Scientists can measure the amount of magma inside a volcano to work out if it will erupt again soon.

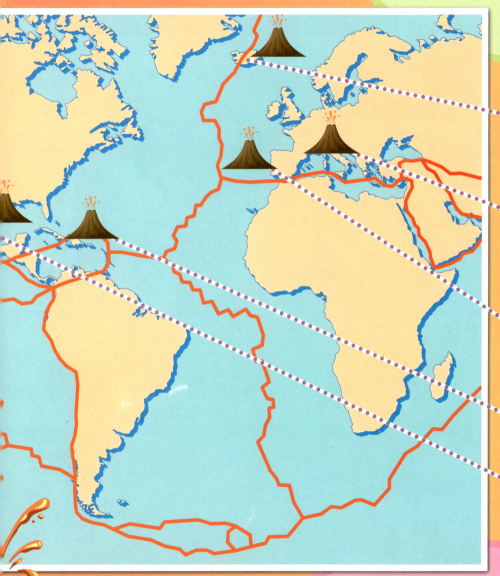

 Eyjafjallajökull (page 23)

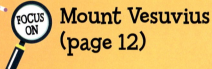 Mount Vesuvius (page 12)

Mount Teide (page 7)

Soufrière Hills (page 29)

Popocatépetl (page 9)

In space

There are also volcanoes on other bodies in space. Io, one of Jupiter's moons, has hundreds of volcanoes, some of which shoot lava hundreds of kilometres up into the air.

The Earth's Layers

The structure of the Earth is made up of several layers. During a volcanic eruption, material from inside the Earth comes to the surface.

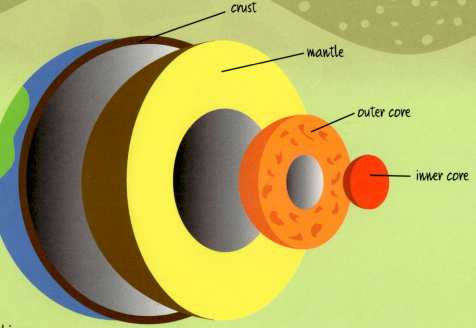

crust

mantle

outer core

inner core

Structure

The structure of the Earth can be divided into four parts. At the centre are the inner and outer cores, which are made from solid and liquid iron and nickel. Then there is the mantle, which contains magma (semi-molten rock). During a volcanic eruption, magma comes to the surface as lava. The outer layer of the Earth is the crust, which is made of solid rock.

Movement

The plates that make up the Earth's surface are always moving. They move a few centimetres every year. This movement is caused by convection currents in the mantle. Hotter magma, which has been heated by the core, rises to the top and then falls down again as it cools. Plates can move towards each other, away from each other or slide past each other.

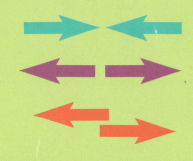

Plates

The Earth's crust is divided into large pieces, known as plates (see map on pages 4–5). Continental plates have land on top. They make up most of the land on Earth. Oceanic plates are found under most of the oceans on Earth. Oceanic plates are denser than continental plates.

Meeting plates

Volcanoes often form at boundaries between continental and oceanic plates. When the plates meet, the denser oceanic plate is pushed under the continental plate and down into the mantle. The solid crust melts in the heat of the mantle and turns into magma.

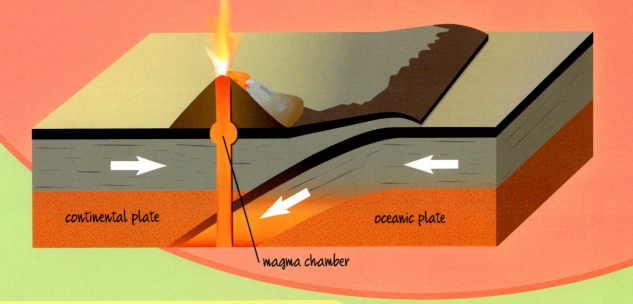

continental plate

oceanic plate

magma chamber

Magma chambers

Magma gathers in huge pools underneath the surface of the Earth, known as magma chambers. Over time, more magma rises into the chamber as more of the oceanic plate is destroyed. Pressure inside the magma chamber builds until it can't hold any more magma. At this point, the magma rises up, causing a volcanic eruption.

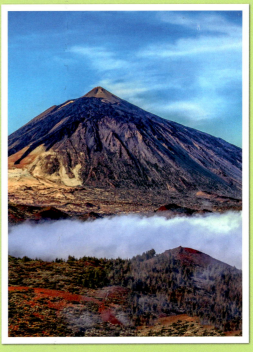

Mount Teide in the Canary Islands, Spain, is a hotspot volcano. Scientists predict that it will probably erupt violently in the future.

Hotspots

In hotspots, the magma in the mantle is much hotter than in the surrounding areas. This hot magma rises to the surface and erupts, creating a volcano. Some hotspots are near plate boundaries, while others are hundreds of kilometres away. Scientists have not yet been able to prove why hotspots exist.

FOCUS ON

The Ring of Fire

The Ring of Fire is a horseshoe-shaped line of volcanoes around the west, north and east coasts of the Pacific Ocean. As well as volcanic activity, there are also many earthquakes in this area.

FACT FILE

LENGTH:
40,000 km

VOLCANOES:
452

COUNTRIES:
Japan, USA, Canada, Chile, The Philippines, Indonesia and many more

Plates

The Ring of Fire is located along different plate boundaries. It marks the place where continental plates meet oceanic plates, such as the huge Pacific plate and the smaller Nazca, Cocos, Philippine and Juan de la Fuca plates. At these boundaries, the oceanic plates are pushed under the continental plates. This process creates volcanoes.

New crust

At the boundaries between the Pacific plate and other oceanic plates, the plates move away from each other. Magma comes up to the surface at these boundaries and hardens to create more crust. Over time, this crust is pushed outwards as more land is created at the boundaries. It replaces the oceanic crust lost under the continental crust around the Ring of Fire. This means that the area of the Pacific Ocean stays roughly the same size.

Volcanoes

Around 75 per cent of all active volcanoes on Earth are located along the Ring of Fire. There are a particularly high number of volcanoes along the western edge of the ring. The volcanoes in Japan alone make up 10 per cent of all of the volcanoes in the world.

Mount Pinatubo

This volcano in the Philippines is located 50 km from Manila, the country's capital. Its eruption in 1991 was the second largest eruption of the 20th century. A 30-km-high ash cloud rose above the volcano, while lava and pyroclastic flows (see page 11) streamed down the mountain. Over 300 people died in the eruption and over 100,000 people lost their homes.

Mount St Helens

This volcano near the west coast of the USA is best known for its massive eruption in 1980. The eruption was set in motion by a huge earthquake, which made one side of the volcano fall away. Next, huge amounts of lava and ash exploded out of the weakened volcano. The high temperatures of the lava melted snow and glaciers on the mountain. The melted water ran downhill, causing huge mudslides that destroyed much of the surrounding countryside.

The Ring of Fire

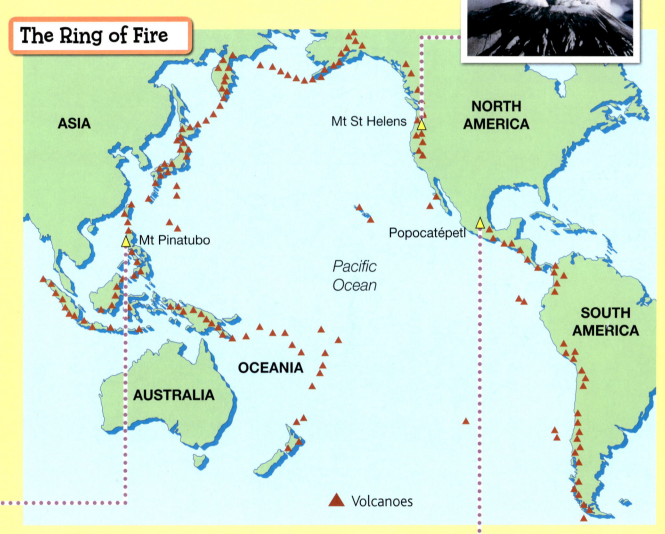

ASIA

NORTH AMERICA

Mt St Helens

Mt Pinatubo

Popocatépetl

Pacific Ocean

OCEANIA

SOUTH AMERICA

AUSTRALIA

▲ Volcanoes

Popocatépetl

Popocatépetl is located in the south of Mexico, around 70 km from its capital, Mexico City. Millions of people live within its eruption zone. It is one of the most active volcanoes in Mexico, but its eruptions are generally mild. However, scientists constantly monitor Popocatépetl for any signs of an explosive eruption that could put local residents at risk.

Eruption

Volcanic eruptions can range in size from a small trickle to a huge explosion. Some have gentle, slow-moving lava, while others include boiling jets of gas and huge ash clouds.

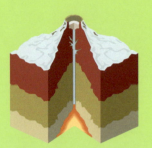   

Internal pressure

Volcanic eruptions happen because of pressure in the magma chamber. As magma from the mantle fills up the chamber, the pressure inside increases. When the chamber is full, this pressure pushes the extra magma up through the main vent – a tube in the centre of the volcano. Some magma may also rise up through smaller vents on the side of the volcano.

Magma

If there is a lot of pressure inside the volcano, some magma is blasted up into the air. This magma can contain large pieces of rock and tiny particles of ash and dust. Liquid magma also flows from the vent and down the sides of the volcano. Once magma reaches the surface, it is known as lava.

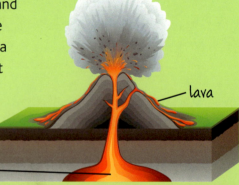

lava

magma

Types of lava

Lava moves in different ways once it leaves a volcano, depending on its temperature and environment. These conditions affect the way in which the lava hardens into rock. The three main types of lava are aa, pahohoe and pillow lava (see page 14).

Aa lava flows very quickly down volcanoes with steep slopes. It picks up pieces of rock from the explosion and the crust as it moves. These rocks get mixed in with the lava as it cools quickly, forming a rough, chunky surface.

Pahoehoe lava moves slowly down a gentle slope. Its slow movement means that the top of the lava can harden into rock as it moves, without breaking up. This gives the hardened lava a smooth surface with a few wrinkles.

Pyroclastic flow

A pyroclastic flow is a mix of rock, ash and very hot gas that moves like a liquid, flowing down the volcano sides at speeds of up to 100 kph. They are extremely dangerous. A human could run away from most lava released by a volcano. However, it is impossible to outrun a pyroclastic flow.

Clouds

Huge clouds of gas, ash and dust are released by eruptions. The gas is poisonous to humans and animals and can be fatal in large amounts. The ash and dust block out light from the Sun until the particles in the air eventually fall to the ground.

The Plinian eruption is named after Pliny, a Roman author who died in the eruption of Mount Vesuvius. The eruption of Vesuvius in CE 79 was a Plinian style eruption.

Types of eruption

Volcano experts have come up with names to describe the different types of volcano eruption. Some of them are named after volcanoes that are typical of a country (Icelandic), or a specific volcano eruption (Strombolian from Mount Stromboli).

Icelandic
• flow from fissures
• not very violent eruptions
• forms large plateaus of volcanic rock

Hawaiian
• runny lava
• forms shield volcanoes (see page 18)
• very little ash

Strombolian
• quite explosive
• expanding gases
• blobs of lava
• thicker lava

Pelean
• very explosive
• pyroclastic flows
• very destructive

Vulcanian
• gas mixed with ash
• huge dark clouds

Plinian
• most violent
• huge column of boiling gas and rock, like a rocket launch
• very high clouds
• pyroclastic flows

Mount Vesuvius

Mount Vesuvius is an active volcano near the city of Naples, Italy. Its most famous eruption took place in CE 79 and destroyed the Roman city of Pompeii.

Formation

Italy is one of the most volcanically active areas in Europe. Its volcanoes are formed by the collision of the African and Eurasian plates. Mount Vesuvius developed on top of the caldera of Mount Somma, an earlier, collapsed volcano. Its tall peak was created by layers of ash and lava from its eruption in CE 79.

FACT FILE

🌍 LOCATION:
Italy

🌋 SHAPE/ERUPTION TYPE:
Somma-stratovolcano/Plinian

🌋 STATUS:
Active

↑ HEIGHT:
1,281 m

The large cone of Mount Vesuvius is partially surrounded by the caldera created by the collapse of Mount Somma.

Early signs

It was a huge surprise for the residents of Pompeii and Herculaneum when Mount Vesuvius erupted on 24 August CE 79. From reading eyewitness accounts, we know that there were some earthquakes before the eruption, caused by moving magma. Today, we know that earthquakes can be a warning sign of an eruption. However, the Romans did not know this and so they were caught totally unaware.

Roman settlements

In the 1st century CE, the Roman settlements of Herculaneum and Pompeii were located at the base of Mount Vesuvius. Herculaneum was a small seaside town, while Pompeii was a large city with up to 15,000 inhabitants. Pompeii was filled with shops, bars and businesses. The towns' residents didn't know that Mount Vesuvius was still active, as it hadn't erupted for nearly 900 years.

Eruption

At the beginning of Mount Vesuvius' eruption, ash and pumice rained down from the sky. A giant ash cloud blocked out the sun and the entire area went dark. People in Pompeii and Herculaneum started to panic. Some ran away, while others took shelter inside buildings.

Deadly flow

At around midnight, the most deadly phase of the eruption began. Scorching pyroclastic flows made up of ash, gas and rock started to rush down the sides of the volcano, at speeds of over 100 kph. The flows covered the nearby towns of Pompeii and Herculaneum. The towns' buildings and residents were buried under liquid rock and ash.

20 metres – *depth of stone and ash that covered Herculaneum*

5 metres – *depth of stone and ash that covered Pompeii*

Deaths

We don't know exactly how many people died during the CE 79 eruption of Mount Vesuvius. So far, archaeologists have found the remains of around 1,500 people. Survivors did not return to the area after the eruption. There have been no settlements built there since.

This is a plaster cast of someone who died in the eruption. When the pyroclastic flows covered the town, bodies were trapped in the ash. When the bodies decomposed, they left a perfect space in the ash. This space was filled with plaster to make this model.

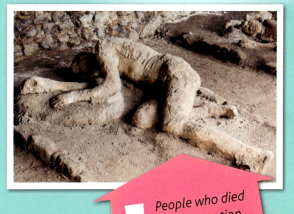

People who died in the eruption were killed instantly by the extremely high temperatures of over 300 °C!

Historical remains

The archaeological remains of Pompeii were discovered in the late 16th century. The rock and ash have preserved many details of life during Roman times. Archaeologists have discovered houses, workshops and restaurants, and even loaves of bread and ancient graffiti! We have learned a lot about life in ancient Roman towns from the remains.

Underwater Volcanoes

Around 80 per cent of volcanic eruptions on Earth take place deep underwater. We are only just starting to learn about these volcanoes thanks to new underwater exploration technology.

Location

Many underwater volcanoes are found at boundaries between ocean plates, where the plates move away from each other. Magma erupts through the gap left by the moving plates and hardens in the cold seawater to form new crust. Over time, a large amount of rock builds up along the plate boundary, forming a raised ridge.

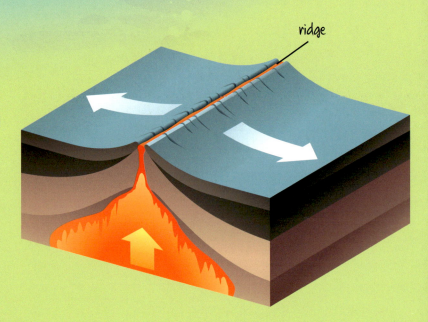

ridge

Eruption

Underwater volcanoes release lava, ash and pieces of rock, just like volcanoes on land. However, the cold water that surrounds underwater volcanoes can cause some of these substances to behave differently. Surrounded by cold water, lava cannot flow far from the volcano before it cools down. In shallow water, the heat from the eruption creates columns of steam that rise out of the water.

Pillow lava

When magma is released into the ocean, it can form pillow lava. This type of lava has a spherical shape. Pillow lava is formed because the outside of the lava quickly hardens in the cool water. Meanwhile, more molten lava flows into the centre of the ball of lava, blowing it up like a balloon.

These balls of pillow lava are on the bed of the Pacific Ocean, near to the Galápagos Islands.

Islands

If an underwater eruption is very violent or takes place in relatively shallow water, the hardened layers of lava that it creates can, over time, rise above sea level. This creates islands. Iceland is an example of an island formed by volcanic activity. It is found on the Mid-Atlantic Ridge, where lava flows from the boundary between two oceanic plates. Iceland is also a volcanic hotspot area, which means that it has even more volcanic activity than a standard plate boundary.

Hydrothermal vents

Jets of mineral-rich water, known as hydrothermal vents, appear in underwater volcanic areas where seawater comes into contact with magma. They happen when cold seawater travels down through cracks in the seabed, and is heated underground by hot magma. When it reaches a high temperature, the hot seawater bursts back up through the seabed as a vent.

Giant tube worms and many other species of living things are found around hydrothermal vents. This is because the mineral-rich water attracts bacteria, which the living things feed on.

Studying underwater volcanoes

Scientists monitor underwater volcanoes with robots that travel through the water like a torpedo, capturing many high-resolution images of the seafloor. They study these images to learn more about the way in which underwater volcanoes erupt. From this research, scientists have recently learned that most underwater volcanoes are very young and formed within the last 4,000 years.

15

Volcanic Rock

Volcanoes play an important role in the rock cycle. When lava from volcanoes hardens, it forms a type of rock called igneous rock.

Types of rock

Igneous rock is one of three main types of rock. The other kinds are sedimentary rock and metamorphic rock. Each type of rock is formed at a different stage of the rock cycle.

The rock cycle

Rocks on Earth do not stay the same forever. They are constantly being broken down and made into new rocks in a process known as the rock cycle. It takes millions of years for rocks to pass through the rock cycle. They travel from inside the Earth to the surface and then back down again. Rocks change type as they move through the rock cycle.

Igneous rock

When magma reaches the Earth's surface through cracks or volcanic eruptions, it cools down and hardens into igneous rock. Igneous rock can also form under the Earth's crust, when magma cools down under the surface. This underground igneous rock is often pushed back down into the mantle by tectonic forces. The heat from the Earth's core melts the igneous rock and it forms magma again.

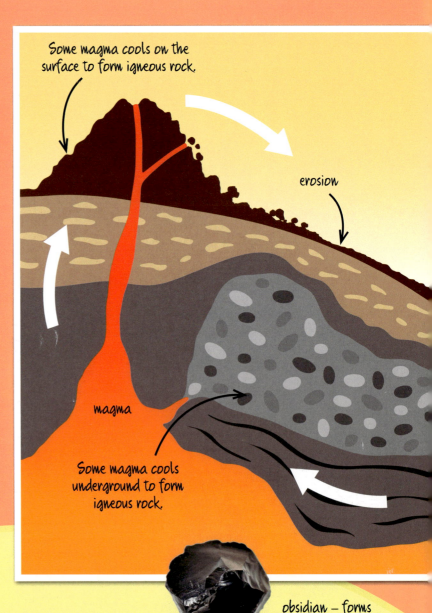

Some magma cools on the surface to form igneous rock.

erosion

magma

Some magma cools underground to form igneous rock.

obsidian – forms above the ground

basalt – forms above the ground

granite – forms under the ground

Erosion and transportation

Rocks on the surface of the Earth are eroded and broken down into smaller pieces by wind, water and pressure. Some very small rock fragments (sediment) fall into rivers and are transported to the lakes and the sea.

Sedimentary rock often contains

fossils

of plants and animals, which were trapped in the layers as they formed.

Sedimentary rock

Very small pieces of rock in lakes and the ocean sink to the bottom, along with salt crystals, sand and tiny particles of bones and shells. Over time, they create layers. When a new layer forms on top of an old layer, the weight of the new layer pushes down the old layers and the particles stick together. After millions of years, the sediment is compacted together into sedimentary rock.

limestone

chalk

sandstone

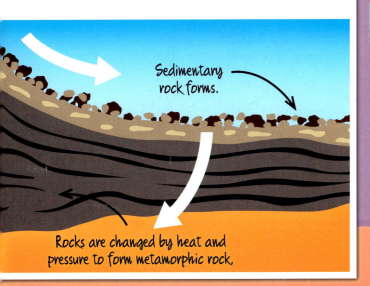

Sedimentary rock forms.

Rocks are changed by heat and pressure to form metamorphic rock.

Heat and pressure

Under the Earth's surface, rocks are heated and put under pressure. If a rock is heated to a very high temperature, it can melt into magma. Underground pressure can force some magma to erupt to the surface, where it hardens into igneous rock.

limestone (sedimentary) – marble

Metamorphic rock

Some igneous and sedimentary rocks don't melt underground. However, the structure of the crystals inside the rocks is changed by the heat and pressure. The rocks experience a chemical change and become metamorphic rocks. Erosion and the formation of mountains can expose metamorphic rocks and bring them to the surface.

granite (igneous) – gneiss

Shapes of Volcano

The shape and size of a volcano depends on the type and quantity of magma that it contains. The most common shapes of volcano are shield, stratovolcano and cinder cone.

Shield volcanoes

A shield volcano is a large volcano with gentle slopes and several vents. The sides of a shield volcano are made of many thin layers of lava. This shape of volcano is formed by runny lava, which flows very quickly and can cover a large area before it hardens.

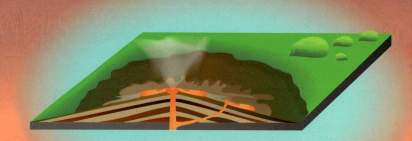

Stratovolcanoes

Large volcanoes with steep slopes are called stratovolcanoes. They usually have more than one vent. The sides of the volcano are made up of layers of ash and hardened lava from previous eruptions. Stratovolcanoes are formed from sticky lava, which cannot flow far before it hardens.

Cinder cone

This is the smallest and most common type of volcano. Cinder cone volcanoes have steep, symmetrical sides and one vent. They usually erupt violently, sending chunks of lava up into the air. The lava hardens in the air and falls down around the vent, building up a cone shape over time.

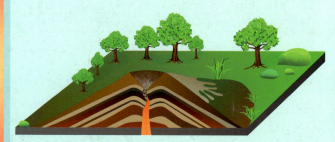

Fissures

In areas where tectonic plates are moving apart, magma rises up along the boundary. The magma hardens and forms a long raised ridge.

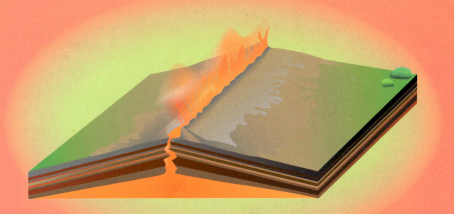

Calderas

If a stratovolcano erupts very violently and ejects most of its magma, the walls of the volcano can collapse, as there is no magma inside to support it. This creates a huge crater, known as a caldera. Over time, the magma chamber underneath the caldera can fill up again and start to erupt. These eruptions will form a new volcano in the centre of the caldera.

Supervolcanoes

A supervolcano is significantly larger and more destructive than a normal volcano. One of the most famous supervolcanoes is in Yellowstone National Park in the USA. It has erupted three times in the past three million years. Its last eruption was 630,000 years ago. This eruption left a massive caldera that measures 55 km by 80 km. Scientists predict that its next eruption will be a global catastrophe.

The magma under the surface of Yellowstone has created many geysers – holes in the ground where hot water and steam are released. The water is boiled underground by the magma before being pushed to the surface by high pressure.

FOCUS ON Mount Fuji

FACT FILE

 LOCATION:
Japan

 SHAPE/ERUPTION TYPE:
Stratovolcano/Plinian

 STATUS:
Active

 HEIGHT:
3,776 m

Mount Fuji is one of the most famous symbols of Japan. It is actually an active volcano, located around 100 km from Tokyo, the capital city of Japan.

Location

There is lots of volcanic activity in Japan. The site of Mount Fuji marks the meeting point of three tectonic plates – the Philippines plate, the Okhotsk plate and the Amur plate.

Eruptions

During the last eruption of Mount Fuji in 1707, a new crater and a smaller second peak were created. Huge amounts of ash were released and fell over areas up to 100 km away from the site of the volcano. Mount Fuji hasn't erupted since, but it is still considered active, as there is magma in its underground chamber.

Formation

The first eruptions on the site of Mount Fuji probably happened around 600,000 years ago. The volcano that you see today is made up of the remains of three volcanoes, which were destroyed during past eruptions. Layers of thick lava and ash from more recent volcanic eruptions covered the remains, giving the volcano its symmetrical cone shape.

Hōei

The smaller peak coming off of Mount Fuji is known as Mount Hōei. It formed during its last eruption in 1707.

FOCUS ON

Mauna Loa

At over 17 km tall, Mauna Loa is the world's largest volcano. Only 4.1 km of its height is above sea level. It measures 5 km underwater and its weight pushes down the crust below it by another 8 km, adding up to over 17 km from base to peak.

Location

The magma in Mauna Loa comes from the Hawaiian hotspot. This hotspot is responsible for the creation of all of the Hawaiian Islands. The hotspot is still releasing lava today, which will eventually form new islands.

Eruptions

We don't have much information about the past eruptions of Mauna Loa as Native Hawaiian people did not record any details. Since records began in the 19th century, it has erupted 33 times. This makes it one of the most active volcanoes on Earth.

FACT FILE

LOCATION:
Hawaii

SHAPE/ERUPTION TYPE:
Shield/Hawaiian

STATUS:
Active

HEIGHT:
4,169 m

Formation

Mauna Loa has been erupting from its base on the seabed for over 700,000 years. By measuring the age of the rocks at sea level on Mauna Loa, scientists have estimated that it probably rose above sea level around 200,000 years ago. It now makes up around half the island of Hawaii. The thin, runny lava that flows from Mauna Loa has given the volcano very gentle slopes.

Mauna Loa

This aerial view of Mauna Loa shows how it dominates the island of Hawaii.

Effects of Volcanoes

Volcanic eruptions can affect the surrounding area, and the rest of the world, in many different ways. They can have an impact on weather, landscape and even global travel.

Climate change

During an eruption, a large amount of sulphur dioxide is released into the atmosphere, where it becomes part of the clouds. Sulphur dioxide makes clouds more reflective. This means that the clouds bounce back more sunlight towards the Sun and away from the Earth. When less sunlight reaches the Earth, temperatures around the world get colder. This is why there is often significant climate change following a major eruption (see page 24).

sulphur dioxide   sunlight (heat)

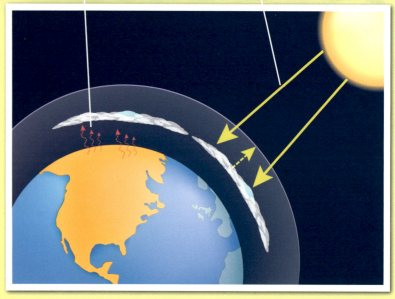

Landscape

The landscape around a volcano is greatly affected after an eruption. Hot lava scorches and destroys anything in its path. Mudflows from melted water can wipe out forests, meadows and fields. Local eco-systems can be damaged, as animals lose their lives and their habitats.

Melting water

The heat from a volcanic eruption can melt snow and ice that have formed at its peak. The melted water flows downhill, mixing with soil and ash from the eruption. If there is a lot of water, it can create fast-moving, dangerous mudflows.

Around 24,000 animals were killed in the Mount St Helen's eruption including:

11,000 hares
6,000 deer
200 black bears
15 mountain lions

FOCUS ON Eyjafjallajökull

Eyjafjallajökull (pronounced ay-yaf-fyat-la-ya-kuh-tel) is an active volcano in Iceland. Its eruption in 2010 created havoc when its ash cloud made it impossible for aeroplanes to fly in Europe.

Clouds

One of the most disruptive consequences of an eruption is the ash cloud that is created. These clouds float through the atmosphere, spreading ash particles far away from the site of the eruption.

FACT FILE

LOCATION:
Iceland

SHAPE/ERUPTION TYPE:
Stratovolcano/Icelandic

STATUS:
Active

HEIGHT:
1,666 m

Eruption

Eyjafjallajökull had been mildly active in the months leading up to its eruption on 14 April 2010. On the day of its eruption, it ejected thousands of tonnes of ash, which created an ash cloud around 9 km high. The cloud was sucked into the jet stream (a strong air current), which spread the ash across Europe.

Aeroplanes

When an aeroplane flies through an ash cloud, its engine sucks in ash particles. These particles damage the engine and can make the aeroplane break down. For this reason, aeroplanes can't fly in areas with high levels of ash in the air.

Cancelled flights

Most of the airspace in Europe had to close as a result of the ash from Eyjafjallajökull. It was too dangerous for aeroplanes to fly for several days. Millions of people had to change their travel plans or extend their holidays.

The eruption of Eyjafjallajökull melted the ice cap that covered the volcano. Steam from the melting ice made the ash cloud even bigger.

Krakatoa

Krakatoa is a volcano on an island off the coast of Indonesia. Its eruption in 1883 was one of the most destructive eruptions in recorded history.

FACT FILE

LOCATION:
Indonesia

SHAPE/ERUPTION TYPE:
Caldera/Plinian

STATUS:
Active

HEIGHT:
approx. 1,800 m

Location

The volcano of Krakatoa is located on a small island between Java and Sumatra – two of the main islands that make up Indonesia. There is lots of volcanic activity in this area, as the Australian Plate is being destroyed under the Eurasian plate.

1883 eruption

Krakatoa had been active for several months before its large eruption. On 26 August 1883, the volcano erupted violently, sending a cloud of ash nearly 30 km high. The next day, there was a catastrophic explosion, which caused two thirds of the island to collapse into the sea. The ash cloud grew to heights of 80 km. The eruption died down during the rest of the day, and by 28 August it had totally finished.

Low temperatures

During the eruption of Krakatoa, a huge amount of sulphur dioxide was released into the atmosphere. The release of this gas lowered the temperature on Earth by 1.2 °C for a year after the explosion. It also increased the amount of rain in some places. The global climate did not return to normal until 1888.

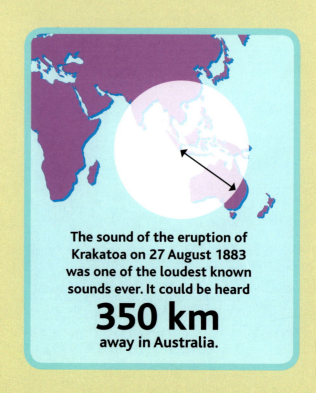

The sound of the eruption of Krakatoa on 27 August 1883 was one of the loudest known sounds ever. It could be heard

350 km
away in Australia.

Sunsets

The ash cloud from the explosion travelled up into the atmosphere and spread around the world. The ash particles reflected different colours of light, which created spectacular bright red and purple sunsets. In some places, the ash particles made the Moon and clouds look blue or green.

New island

In 1927, lava began to erupt out of the sea floor in the same place that Krakatoa had stood before its eruption. By 1930, the lava had reached above sea level. A new volcanic island called Anak Krakatau (Child of Krakatoa) started to form. Anak Krakatau continued to be active throughout the 20th and 21st centuries. It has released so much lava that the volcano now measures 300 m above sea level.

Tsunamis

The force of the collapse of the volcano triggered tsunamis (giant waves). Waves 37 m high reached the coasts of nearby Sumatra and Java, destroying settlements and killing over 36,000 people. Massive waves caused by the eruption travelled as far as South America and Hawaii. Many nearby boats capsized and were destroyed by the waves.

Sertung   181 m

300 m

Anak Krakatau

131 m

Panjang

813 m

Rakata

- ■ previous extent of Krakatoa
- ■ remains of Krakatoa

Anak Krakatau is still erupting today. If it continues to erupt regularly, it will become even taller.

Living near Volcanoes

Living near volcanoes can pose a great danger to humans. However, it can also bring great benefits.

Cities

Many large settlements around the world have developed near volcanoes. The city of Naples in Italy is around 9 km from Mount Vesuvius. Mexico City, Mexico, is within the eruption zone of Popocatépetl. Some cities, such as Edinburgh, have been built on the sites of extinct volcanoes.

1 in 20

people around the world live within the 'danger range' of an active volcano.

Arequipa, the second largest city in Peru, is only 17 km from the volcano, El Misti. The city would be at high risk if El Misti erupted violently.

✗ Cons

Eruption risk

Lava isn't a great threat to humans, as it flows so slowly that most people could outrun it. The main danger during a volcanic eruption is pyroclastic flows, which strike suddenly and violently. Even if humans escape the eruption, lava and pyroclastic flows will damage a settlement and destroy anything in their path.

Gases

Volcanoes produce a lot of steam, which is not dangerous to humans. However, they also release small amounts of carbon monoxide, carbon dioxide and other poisonous gases. This can become dangerous for people who live near constantly active volcanoes, as the small amounts of gas add up over time. Breathing in these gases can lead to breathing problems, headaches and tiredness.

✔ Pros

Fertile soil

After an eruption, the lava and ash break down and mix into the soil. Minerals from the volcanic rock fertilise the soil and make it better for agriculture. Plants grow to be bigger and stronger in fertile volcanic soils, which makes it easier for nearby residents to grow enough food to survive.

Tourism

The dramatic scenery created by volcanoes can attract many tourists. People come to watch active volcanoes with mild eruptions that do not pose a serious threat. Tourism helps to support local economies as it brings money and jobs to the area.

A tourist takes photos of pahoehoe lava in Hawaii. People have been travelling to Hawaii to see volcanoes since the 19th century.

Over **100** million tourists visit volcanoes every year.

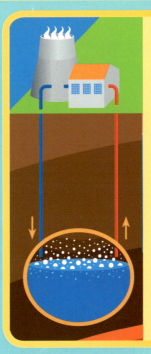

Geothermal energy

Some people in volcanic areas, such as Iceland, use heat energy from volcanoes to create electricity. This is known as geothermal energy. It works by using underground heat to warm water. This creates steam, which turns a turbine. The turbine drives a generator that generates electricity. Geothermal energy is sustainable and doesn't harm the environment.

Predicting Eruptions

Although we still aren't able to predict a volcanic eruption with total accuracy, there are certain signs that suggest that an eruption will happen soon.

Past eruptions

Looking at the frequency of past eruptions is one of the easiest prediction methods. There are historical records that describe many volcanoes and date back hundreds of years. If a volcano erupts every 200 years and the last eruption was 200 years ago, it's likely that there will be another eruption soon. However, we don't have information for volcanoes that erupt less frequently, so this method isn't foolproof.

Heat and gas

The temperature and type of gas found around a volcano also changes right before eruption. We can measure the temperature around volcanoes using thermometers and thermal cameras. Chemical sensors can check for sulphurous gas that suggests an eruption will happen soon.

Earthquakes

An increase in the number of earthquakes in an area can be a sign that an eruption is going to happen. These earthquakes are caused by the movement of magma underground and inside the magma chamber. We can observe earthquakes with a machine called a seismometer.

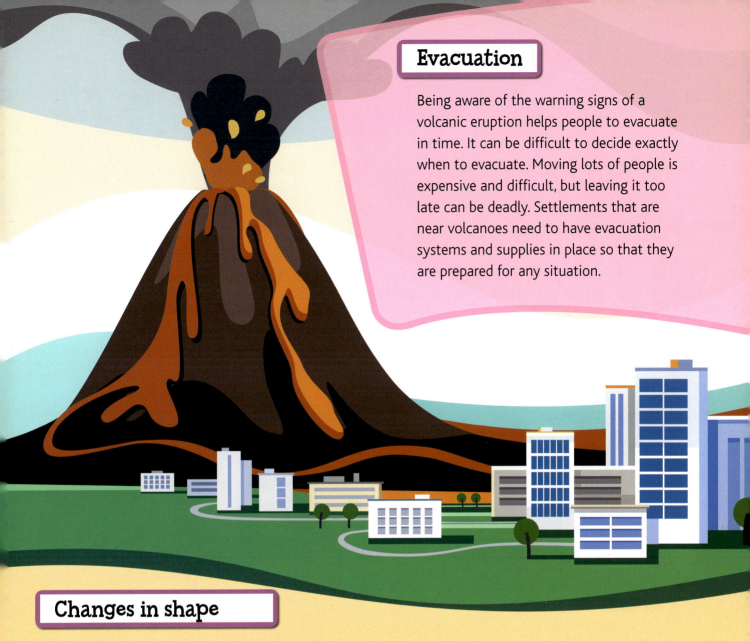

Evacuation

Being aware of the warning signs of a volcanic eruption helps people to evacuate in time. It can be difficult to decide exactly when to evacuate. Moving lots of people is expensive and difficult, but leaving it too late can be deadly. Settlements that are near volcanoes need to have evacuation systems and supplies in place so that they are prepared for any situation.

Changes in shape

When magma builds up under the surface before an eruption, it can change the surface or shape of a volcano. For example, there was a large bulge on the side of Mount St Helens before it erupted in 1980.

Exclusion zone

Some volcanoes are so active that they are a constant danger to humans. An exclusion zone is set up around the volcano where no one can live or build houses. The Soufrière Hills volcano on the island of Montserrat in the Caribbean has been erupting since 1995. Two thirds of the island's population left between 1995 and 2000. Half the island is still an exclusion zone, which no one can enter.

The pyroclastic flows from Soufrière Hills still cover large areas of Montserrat.

Glossary

active an active volcano erupts regularly

caldera a very large empty basin that is left when a volcano collapses after an eruption

continental plate a large piece of the Earth's crust that lies under a continent and along some coasts

convection current movement caused by hot liquid rising and cool liquid falling

crust the outer layer of the Earth

dense the molecules in a dense substance are closely compacted together

dormant a dormant volcano is unlikely to erupt soon

erosion the gradual destruction of soil and stone by wind, water and pressure

extinct an extinct volcano will never erupt again

fertilise to add something to soil that makes plants grow well

glacier a large amount of ice that moves slowly

hotspot an area of the Earth where the magma is much hotter than usual

igneous rock a type of rock made from hardened lava

lava hot, melted rock outside a volcano

magma hot, melted rock inside a volcano

mantle the layer of the Earth underneath the crust

metamorphic rock a type of rock that has been chemically changed by heat and pressure in the mantle

molten melted

oceanic plate a large piece of the Earth's crust that lies under the ocean

peak the top point of a mountain

plate boundary the place where two tectonic plates meet

pyroclastic flow a fast-moving flow of ash, lava and gas

sea level the height of the sea where it meets the land

sedimentary rock a type of rock made from layers of compacted sediment

settlement a place where humans have settled and live permanently, such as a town

tectonic plate a section of the Earth's crust

tsunami an extremely large wave created by the movement of the Earth

Test yourself!

1 Name three countries located on the Ring of Fire.

2 What's the difference between magma and lava?

3 Which type of eruption is the most violent?

4 Which Roman cities did Mount Vesuvius destroy?

5 Which type of volcano is steeper – shield or stratovolcano?

6 What is the world's largest volcano?

7 How tall was the ash cloud from Eyjafjallajökull?

8 What are two positive effects of volcanoes?

Check your answers on page 32.

Further reading

Volcanoes and Earthquakes (Where on Earth?)
Susie Brooks (Wayland, 2015)

Volcano Disasters (Catastrophe!)
John Hawkins (Franklin Watts, 2014)

Volcanoes (Our Earth in Action)
Chris Oxlade (Franklin Watts, 2014)

Websites

Read more about volcanoes at the following websites:

www.bbc.co.uk/science/earth/natural_disasters/volcano

www.dkfindout.com/uk/earth/volcanoes/

www.natgeokids.com/uk/discover/geography/physical-geography/volcano-facts/

Index

Answers

1 Japan, USA, Canada, Chile, the Philippines, Indonesia , New Zealand, Mexico, Peru and more

2 Magma is under the Earth's surface and lava is above the Earth's surface.

3 Plinian

4 Pompeii and Herculaneum

5 Stratovolcano

6 Mauna Loa

7 9 km

8 Fertile soil, geothermal energy and tourism

GEOGRAPHICS
Series contents lists

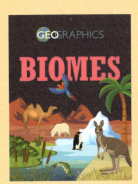

Biomes
- What is a Biome? • Forests
- Yosemite • Rainforests • The Amazon Rainforest • Grasslands and Savannahs • The Serengeti
- Deserts • The Sahara Desert
- Tundra and Ice • Antarctica
- Oceans • The Great Barrier Reef
- Rivers and Lakes • The Nile River

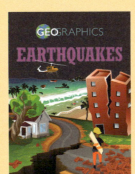

Earthquakes
- What is an Earthquake?
- Tectonic Plates • Plate Boundaries and Faults • San Francisco 1906
- Measuring Earthquakes
- Earthquake Hazards • Peru 1970
- Earthquakes and Buildings
- Rescue and Relief • Nepal 2015
- Preparing for Earthquakes
- Tsunamis • Japan 2011

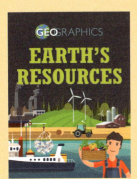

Earth's Resources
- What are Resources? • Mining
- Wood • Plastic • Recycling and Rubbish • Agriculture • GM Crops
- Fishing • North Sea Fishing
- Recycling • Fossil Fuels
- Sustainable Energy • Eco-cities

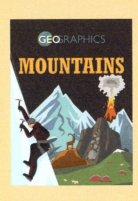

Mountains
- What is a Mountain?
- Moving Plates • Fold and Block Mountains • Volcanic Mountains
- The Andes • Changing Mountains
- The Alps • Climate • Biomes
- The Rocky Mountains • People and Mountains • The Himalayas
- Mountain Resources
- The Appalachian Mountains

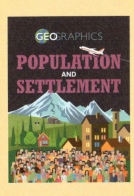

Population and Settlement
- What are Population and Settlement? • Distribution and Density • Population Growth
- Overpopulation • Population Structure • Uganda and Japan
- Migration • UK Migration
- Settlement Sites • Athens
- Settlement Layout • Manila
- Changing Settlements

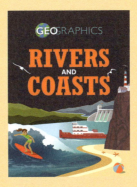

Rivers and Coasts
- Rivers and Coasts • River Structure • The Ganges River
- River Erosion • River Formations
- The Colorado River • Types of Coasts • The UK Coast • Changing Coasts • Arches and Stacks • The Twelve Apostles • People and Water • The Three Gorges Dam
- Flooding • Venice

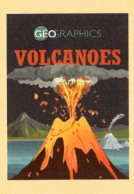

Volcanoes
- What are Volcanoes?
- Formation • The Ring of Fire
- Stratovolcanoes • Mount Fuji
- Shield Volcanoes • Mauna Kea
- Calderas and Cinder Cones
- Eruption • Mount Vesuvius
- Lava • Underwater Volcanoes
- Dormant and Extinct Volcanoes

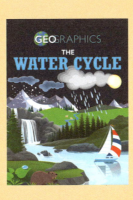

The Water Cycle
- What is the Water Cycle?
- Our Blue Planet • Evaporation
- The Amazon Rainforest
- Condensation • Clouds
- Precipitation • Rainfall • Rain in the Himalayas • Accumulation
- River Basins • The Mississippi River
- Water Stores • Polar Ice Caps
- Humans and the Water Cycle